How to Graduate from College
Debt-Free

John D. Lane IV

iUniverse, Inc.
Bloomington

How to Graduate from College Debt-Free

Copyright © 2011 John D. Lane IV

All rights reserved. No part of this book may be used or reproduced by any means, graphic, electronic, or mechanical, including photocopying, recording, taping or by any information storage retrieval system without the written permission of the publisher except in the case of brief quotations embodied in critical articles and reviews.

The information, ideas, and suggestions in this book are not intended to render professional advice. Before following any suggestions contained in this book, you should consult your personal accountant or other financial advisor. Neither the author nor the publisher shall be liable or responsible for any loss or damage allegedly arising as a consequence of your use or application of any information or suggestions in this book.

iUniverse books may be ordered through booksellers or by contacting:

iUniverse
1663 Liberty Drive
Bloomington, IN 47403
www.iuniverse.com
1-800-Authors (1-800-288-4677)

Because of the dynamic nature of the Internet, any Web addresses or links contained in this book may have changed since publication and may no longer be valid. The views expressed in this work are solely those of the author and do not necessarily reflect the views of the publisher, and the publisher hereby disclaims any responsibility for them.

Any people depicted in stock imagery provided by Thinkstock are models, and such images are being used for illustrative purposes only.

Certain stock imagery © Thinkstock.

ISBN: 978-1-4620-1262-6 (pbk)
ISBN: 978-1-4620-1260-2 (ebk)

Library of Congress Control Number: 2011905764

Printed in the United States of America

iUniverse rev. date: 4/21/2011

Dedication

Talk to anyone who has made it in business, professional sports or the top of their respective field and they probably had someone who had a tremendous impact on their life and played an intricate part in their being the success they are today. Perhaps it was a teacher, coach or someone they could look up to and trust to lead them down the path to success.

Although I have not traveled far down this elusive path, I have had many mentors who have influenced the route I am traveling. Without their guidance and words of encouragement none of this would have been possible.

I dedicate this book to them in hopes that the lessons I learned from them could be passed along to many other students so they can apply the principles in their own life.

Acknowledgments

A special thank you to:

My Mother and Father, John and Laura Lane, for instilling in me the principles of financial responsibility at a young age

My Grandparents for always being there to support all my endeavors

My Sister, Danielle Lane, for creating the images in the book as well as Alex Warschauer for the photography

My Mentors and Friends for the encouragement to pursue my ambitions

Contents

Chapter One — 1
Dreams Count

Chapter Two — 5
Dream Transformer

Chapter Three — 9
Converting Dreams to Goals

Chapter Four — 21
Work It

Chapter Five — 25
Personal Declaration

Chapter Six — 31
Adjust

Chapter Seven — 35
Persist

"Stop assuming your parents will pay for your college education."
—John D. Lane IV

My name is John Daniel Lane IV; my friends call me *Johnny D*. In June 2007, I earned a bachelor's degree in business administration, with an option in economics. CSUEB is a four-year, state university where the graduation rate is around 55 percent, and those who do graduate take an average of six years to do so. I did it in four years, made some good friends along the way, and had some fun times; but most importantly, I graduated without creating any debt for my parents or myself.

What I did wasn't so unique that anyone going to college couldn't do it. However, I noticed that few students did. Most of my college friends accrued debt in the form of student loans and credit cards, thus graduating with tens of thousands of dollars of debt on their backs or their parents. I'm not sure why they did this. I'd have to say from talking with friends today, some of whom I've known since middle school, it was just that they never thought about graduating without any loans to pay off. Well, I say, think about it, set a goal, and work to attain it.

Graduating without debt gives you the character and freedom to choose a career after you have earned your degree. Character comes from learning and applying the principles in this book, and freedom comes from having money in the bank and being financially debt-free. You will owe a huge debt of gratitude to your family, friends, and the organizations that took an interest in your graduating without acquiring any financial debt.

Avoiding financial debt while gaining a degree is what this book is about. Debt is bad for you, for me, for our local and national governments, and for the world economy. The sooner you learn how to graduate from college debt-free and begin to work toward that goal, the greater success you will have in achieving it.

I believe that the younger you start planning and thinking about college finances, the better the odds that you will actually graduate from college, and your life after graduation will be easier. That's why I'm writing this book, and I hope that's why you are reading it.

This book is organized into chapters and miniworkshops, which introduce a concept, offer examples, and give a few related personal stories. I encourage you to read every chapter and do every exercise completely before moving on. When you have finished, go back and read the entire book from cover to cover at least once a year. After doing so, you will start moving toward your newly determined goal of graduating from college debt free.

I am not suggesting that success will come without work or using some newfound disciplines; but if you read these chapters and work through the exercises provided in each chapter, some level of success will be yours. This technique has been proven in science, business, religion, relationships, and many other areas of life. It has helped me to achieve many of my personal goals, such as starting my own business, YES Group Marketing, when I was sixteen, obtaining my real estate license when I was eighteen, and earning a business degree in less than four years debt-free.

Chapter One
Dreams Count

Webster's Definition
Dreams: A series of mental images, ideas, and emotions occurring in certain stages of sleep. A state of trance. A wild hope or fantasy. An ambition.

My Definition
Dreams: Thoughts that stir up positive or negative emotions.

Dreams are a gift that allows us to expand our thinking in order to better our lives and those of others. The ability to dream helps us develop our future. We wouldn't have been given the power to dream if it were not possible to achieve our dreams. Consider that everything you dream you might actually attain. Don't be afraid to reach for the stars, because dreams do count.

Mankind dreamed of flying long before Orville and Wilbur Wright took flight in 1903, and now through such dreams and the advance of technology and science, we fly better than birds. Early explorers dreamed of walking on the moon, and now NASA collaborates with other nations maintaining the International Space Station, where scientists live 220 miles above the earth for months at a time.

Assignment #1:

Get a sheet of binder paper and a pencil. At the top of your paper, write down the word "Dreams." Make a list of at least twenty dreams you'd like to fulfill in your lifetime.

Answering a few of these questions may help you make your list.
1. What is your dream vacation?
2. What is your dream car?
3. What does your dream mate look like?
4. What does your dream family look like?
5. What is your dream career?
6. Where is your dream home?
7. What does your dream home look like?
8. What does your dream lifestyle feel like?
9. What is the college experience of your dreams?

You can write anything on this piece of paper. Phrase your dream statements as though you will achieve your dream, not just that you want it. For example: "I will vacation in Paris." Let your imagination run wild. Date and file this dream list in a three-ring binder for use in later assignments.

If you had difficulty completing this exercise, try reading more to stimulate your mind. Try different types of material, such as the daily news, travel magazines, biographies, and classics, instead of just school texts and comic books. Another way to broaden your imagination is to write daily. Spending as little as ten minutes each day journaling your thoughts will encourage creative thinking. Go to the library, pick up any book that catches your eye, and just read. Our brains love to expand the stories we read, adding images and sound, developing our imaginations. Reading will also limit the time you spend watching television, playing video games, or just surfing the World Wide Web.

Chapter Two
Dream Transformer

Webster's Definition
Transform: To alter markedly the appearance or form. To change the nature, function, or condition of something.

My Definition
Transform: Cars that can change into robots.

As I mentioned in the last chapter, dreams count. They count because they carry emotion and build desire. Bad dreams carry the emotions of fear and rejection, while good dreams carry the emotions of cheer and desire. In this chapter, you will take your good dreams and transform them into the fuel needed to achieve a goal that you may not have given any previous thought to: to graduate from college debt-free.

When I was eight years old, there was a movie I watched a dozen times. It was about a captive, performing whale named Willy that a young boy let free; the movie was appropriately named *Free Willy*. I loved that movie and dreamed that when I grew up, I would become a whale trainer. My parents said that it would be a great job, but I would have to get a college degree as no one would let me handle a whale without one. That's my first memory of knowing that I would get a degree.

Over the years, my dream careers changed, but the necessity of a degree never did. When I was passionate about being a ballplayer, I was told I needed to go to college to earn a degree and get scouted by a major league team. When I became interested in girls, they said the best girls are in college, and I needed to earn a degree to attract them. When I decided I wanted to be a CEO, I knew I needed a degree in business. I received my MBA in June 2010.

Assignment #2:

Get your binder out again because you'll be doing a lot of writing. Look at your dreams list. Did you answer the question about your dream college experience? Did it sound like a trick? It was. So if you wrote that you want to go to a party school, prepare to use that dream to fuel your goal of graduating debt-free.

At the top of a fresh sheet of binder paper, write the word "Affirmations." Just below that, write out, "I will graduate from college debt-free." From your dreams list, identify ten dreams that really excite you—the ten that you would most likely accomplish if you just knew how. List these ten dreams in order of priority and tag the statement "I will graduate from college debt-free" at the beginning of each dream.

By coupling your dreams to your newfound goal of graduating from college debt-free, the emotional ties you already have with the dreams will give your newfound goal great emotional power. Make sure to start your affirmations with "I." For example: "I will graduate from college debt-free, which will allow me the opportunity to go on an extended vacation to explore the ancient ruins of Machu Picchu during the summer after I graduate."

Now that you have this list of affirmations, make a copy to keep with you, and put the original in your binder. Read your affirmations in the morning and again before you go to sleep at night until you've memorized them. Rewriting them will help with the memory process. Once you've taken these affirmations to heart, the desires that are associated with your ten dreams will be transformed into one new goal: to graduate from college debt-free.

Chapter Three
Converting Dreams to Goals

Webster's Definition
Goal: The objective toward which an endeavor is directed. The finish line of a race. The score rewarded for such an act.

My Definition
Goal: The uprights at each end of a football field.

Goals are different than dreams. Whereas dreams are emotional, goals are SMART. They are:
- Specific
- Measurable
- Attainable
- Realistic
- Time-Sensitive

They should be monitored to determine if you're progressing, slacking off, or moving in the right direction. You may even determine that your goals need to be changed to meet your true desires.

I wish I could tell you all you need to do is write down your dreams, remember them, and you will succeed, but that is not the case. The only place success comes before work is in the dictionary. Writing down your dreams and remembering them will make it easier for you to achieve them. As a matter of fact, the process will inspire you to work harder and smarter. Adding the elements of work and a written commitment will turn your dreams to reality.

Know which end of the field your goal is on.

Assignment #3:

Now that you've adopted the big dream/goal of graduating from college debt-free, it's time to convert that big goal to smaller, bite-size goals. This will require setting subgoals in many areas, such as academics, extracurricular activities, work, savings, and relationships, to name a few. You may have more or fewer areas, but we're going to work with these five as an example.

Get six new sheets of binder paper. At the top of the first sheet, write out your #1 big goal: "I will graduate from college debt-free." Think about that for a moment. How long are you planning on taking to graduate? I chose four years because I knew the more time it took to graduate, the more it would cost. On the second line, write down the month and year you will graduate. Now, in the space beneath your #1 big goal, write a statement dealing with each of the areas in which you have subgoals. See the next page for an example.

#1 Big Goal: I will graduate from college debt-free.

Completion date: June 2015

- Academics: I will take the classes and earn the grades necessary in high school and college in order to graduate from college debt-free.
- Extracurricular activities: I will participate in extracurricular activities in high school and college in order to graduate from college debt-free.
- Work: I will work to help pay for college while in high school and college in order to graduate from college debt-free.

- Savings: I will save and invest my money while in high school and college in order to graduate from college debt-free.
- Relationships: I will establish and strengthen my relationships while in high school and college in order to graduate from college debt-free.

At the top of the second sheet, write Academic Goal; beneath it, write your academic commitment. Use my example or one of your own. Below the goal, put the date this goal needs to be completed by. Most of your completion dates will probably be the year you expect to graduate from high school or sooner. See the next page for an example.

Additional statements within your goal may refer to the academic requirements of classes and grades and how you will go about achieving your goal. For instance, "I will achieve good grades during my high school career." Yes, I said *career*; school is work. You might not get paid today, but if you do a good job, you will get paid well tomorrow. You can earn academic scholarships or grants if you take the right classes and get good enough grades. Put down the GPA you're shooting for to the right of this statement. I shot for a 4.0; you may try for better. Your academic statement might reflect classes, such as "I will take advanced placement classes." You might include a list that could be checked off, such as AP English, AP statistics, AP history, and so forth.

Academic Goal

I will take the classes and earn the grades in high school necessary to graduate from college debt-free by taking advanced placement classes:
- AP English,
- AP history,
- AP calculus.

I will study 3+ hours a night and keep in touch with my counselor on a weekly basis in order to learn of any academic scholarships for which I can apply.

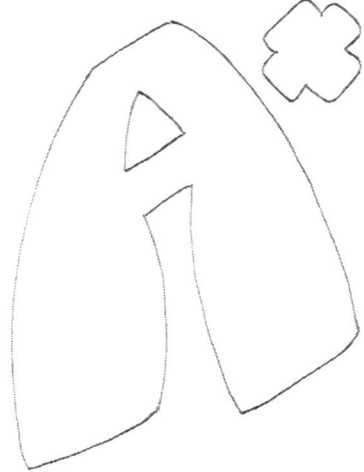

Completion date: June 2011   GPA goal: 4.0

On the next sheet (see example on next page), repeat the process with your extracurricular goal category. Remember to add a completion date. Next, write down a statement that lists extracurricular activities, such as volunteering, involvement on the debate team, student government, music, or my favorite—sports, and how you will accomplish them. Your statement may be something like, "I will become president of the student body." You might include in this statement, "by my junior year." Extracurricular activities differentiate you from the other students who will be applying to the same college and for the same scholarships that you are. The more the better, but don't get overwhelmed. The quality of your participation is as important as the number of activities in which you are involved.

Extracurricular Goal

I will participate in extracurricular activities that will help me graduate from college debt-free, such as volunteering once a week at the Community Food Bank, joining the drama club, and playing the drums in the school band. I will also run for student body office by my sophomore year.

Completion date: June 2011

At the top of the fourth blank sheet, repeat the process with your Work Goal category. To graduate debt-free, you will probably work from the time you finish this book to the time you graduate from college, unless you're fortunate enough to have a rich uncle! But if you start working part-time now, you won't have to work full-time through college. In this case, I used a monthly income goal instead of a completion date.

Your statement might look like, "I will work a part-time job through high school." Include how many hours per week you will work. Or, if flexibility is a priority, you can start your own service like I did. Your statement could be something like this: "I will cut my neighbor's lawn or babysit to earn money." Put down the number of customers you will serve each week, for instance; five lawns a week, or the income you expect to earn.

Work Goal

I will work while in high school in order to graduate from college debt-free, cutting lawns and babysitting to earn money. I will pursue finding a regular part-time job for the weekends or after school.

Hours per week: 10 hours per week
Income goal: $500.00 a month

On sheet five, repeat the process with your Savings Goal category. This is easy! Include the lump sum you'll need, with a completion date.

The next statement might be something like this: "I will save to pay for my college expenses." Put down how much money you want to save each month, for example; $350.00. The sooner you start saving, the more you will be able to save. Not only that, but the more interest you will earn on it.

Savings Goal

I will save money while in high school in order to graduate from college debt-free by putting aside 75 percent of whatever I earn. After seeking prudent advice on investing, I will invest where it will earn the most interest.

Amount needed to save: $350.00 per month

On the last blank sheet, repeat the process with your Relationships Goal category. As before, put a completion date. Relationships are important in love, war, politics, business, and graduating from college debt-free. It takes effort to create them, maintain them, and benefit from them. Strengthen your relationships with your parents, grandparents, aunts and uncles, parents' friends, friends and their parents, counselors, pastors, and teachers because they are all crucial in your journey toward graduating from college debt-free. Any one of them can help you cover portions of your education, provide a job, give a letter of recommendation, or direct you to a scholarship.

There are books written on building meaningful relationships. Your statement might look like this: "I will keep in contact with my counselor/aunt/mentor." Include *how*, for example, "by visiting them on a weekly basis." Make sure they know your goal is to graduate from college debt-free. You will be surprised how your circle of acquaintances will help you attain your goals.

Relationship Goal

I will establish and strengthen my relationships while in both high school and college in order to graduate from college debt-free by keeping in touch with friends and relatives and close family. I will keep them informed of my goal to graduate from college debt-free and follow up with suggestions they may have as to possible contacts, sources of scholarships, etc.
Completion date: Ongoing

Put your list of goals and subgoals in a binder for regular monitoring. As time goes on, you will add to them, take from them, and adjust them as you continue to pursue your main goal, to graduate from college debt-free.

Personal Anecdote
Saving for College

Entrepreneurial spirit was encouraged by my parents. They would rather I was out selling used golf balls and lemonade on a hot summer day to the golfers than be cooped up in the house blasting the air-conditioning and watching *Fresh Prince* and MTV all day long.

Tennis shoes are an expensive commodity. After I ran my way through a few pairs of these staples of the playground, my parents thought it best to give me my first lesson in understanding budgeting for items I wanted and felt I needed. This meant instead of them shelling out $100.00 for a pair of Jordans every six months, they would give me an allowance and allow me to justify my own purchases of such items. I learned how to save my money and, even more importantly, be frugal about my spending habits. Once given the responsibility of buying my own shoes, I oddly enough cared for them more and no longer bought Jordans.

In my family, I became known as Squeaky, because I was thrifty with my money. They say I am so tight I squeak when I walk. I learned the difference between a want and a need. Clothing, shelter, and food are our needs. Luxuries are those Jordans, that mansion, and eating filet mignon. In order to satisfy my wants and desires, I learned I must work for them. Some might argue that I was a little too stingy, but hey, it paid off in the end. I eventually carried the experiences of managing my allowance and saving the money I earned from selling golf balls into saving and budgeting for college life.

By learning to live below your means, you will be able to make better decisions about your financial future. Don't let the pressures of your peers and people you associate with influence your decisions on the basis of status alone.

Chapter Four
Work It

Webster's Definition
Work: Physical or mental effort or activity directed toward the production or accomplishment of something: labor, employment, job.

My Definition
Work: Attaining small goals that will lead to achieving larger goals.

In order to get into college, you must earn good grades and good SAT and ACT test scores. You may already know what you need to work on to accomplish this, but let's review some of the finer points of getting good grades.

- Number one is your involvement in the classroom. Sit in the front of the room; ask questions instead of texting with your friends. Learn to take good notes and participate in classroom projects. All these actions are important habits to develop in order to earn good grades.
- Number two is your effort outside the classroom. Do your homework on a timely basis, read ahead whenever possible, get involved with study groups when available, ask your teacher for after-school help, get tutored if you need it, take SAT and ACT preparatory workshops, and tell your parents if you need help.

My junior year in high school was difficult because I was taking a trigonometry class that I felt was out of my league. I always believed that I could succeed in any class I put my mind to, but for some reason the concepts weren't making sense. I told my parents, and they suggested that I get a tutor. After a few sessions, I started to understand and my grade improved. If I hadn't asked, I would never have gotten the help I needed.

Consider taking college courses at your local junior college while still in high school. Summer classes are usually less expensive at a junior college. Make sure the units are transferable to the college you plan on attending, so you do not have to take the class again.

I took an American government class one summer. My family went on a Hawaiian vacation for a week, and there I was on the beach diving into a political science textbook. I got an A in that class and earned four units as well as a suntan.

What we'll cover in the rest of this chapter are the areas you should focus your work efforts on to graduate from college debt-free. Remember, the sooner you start, the better. A good work ethic consists of showing up on time and fully involving yourself with the task at hand until the end of the shift or completion of the job. This means you cannot be late, tired, or out-of-it in any way. Ask questions if you're not sure what is expected. Know what you're working toward and the effect or outcome your employer or customer is looking for.

As a teenager, finding a job that pays well and leaves you time to do homework and have a bit of social life is really not that difficult. Businesses like fast-food restaurants and retail stores are always looking to hire and will usually work around your school schedule.

The biggest problem is that teenagers often seem to feel their parents should take care of everything, and if they work at all, the money should be theirs to spend!

Consider this: it feels good to get paid by someone else for what you do, and it feels good to have money that you have earned in the bank. Don't assume that your parents should pay for your college education.

Assignment #4:

Get a work permit and a part-time job and start saving your paycheck to offset your college expenses or start a service business. The work experience will look great on your college application as well as on your job resume.

Chapter Five
Personal Declaration

Webster's Definition

Declaration: An explicit or formal announcement or statement. Such a statement in written form. The final bid of a hand in some card games.

My Definition

Declaration: A personal jingle whose purpose is to evoke action-driving emotion.

Now you get to make your own commercial—one that motivates you and your friends and family to buy into your #1 big goal, the goal of graduating from college debt-free.

Marketing and advertising is a multi-billion-dollar business. Every company is trying to get you to buy their products or services. They are coming at you from every direction, from television to newspapers to mass mail and billboards; the Internet is fast becoming the largest marketer of goods. No matter what media is used, all have one thing in common: they want to control your thoughts and move you to buy whatever they have to sell.

Now it is time for you to create dialogues, advertisements, mantras, or personal declarations that will motivate you to accomplish your #1 big goal. Here is how you do it.

Assignment #5:

Get a new sheet of binder paper and at the top write Personal Declarations. From the statements that you have for your goals and subgoals, narrow down to the most important three or four sentences. Next, arrange them in a way that you can memorize and recite them with ease and enthusiasm.

A few examples are:
- "I earn excellent grades in school, so that I will be able to get a degree in teaching debt-free."
- "I excel at basketball while keeping a 4.0 GPA, so that I can play and pay my way to a degree in economics."
- "I have many friends and contacts who will help me earn a degree in nursing debt-free."
- "I will get a degree in communications remaining debt-free because I can do anything to which I focus my mind and apply my time."

After you have created your personal declarations, take time to memorize them. Recite them at least five times a day: when you wake up in the morning, at breakfast, lunch, and dinner, and right before you go to sleep at night.

They should become your calling cards, so share them with as many people as possible. You might not believe the jingle at first, but with continued repetition, your personal declarations will eventually become you and in time you will become them. After you've mastered a couple of personal jingles, consider creating some more.

Personal Anecdote
How I Earned My Gas Money

When I turned sixteen, I used a portion of my savings to buy my first car. My parents thought I should buy an inexpensive car, but it was my money. I had saved more than $10,000 by this time and felt I was well on track to having enough money to get through college debt-free. The car I wanted was a 1979 Porsche that my mom had owned since before I was born. Looking back, I should have listened to my parents and let them sell it to someone who could afford to care for a vintage car. Now I had the responsibility of paying for gas and upkeep on a very maintenance-intense car! Oh well, shouldn't dwell on the past.

For years I'd been working for my dad, handing out his real estate flyers for about ten cents apiece. Talk about child labor! I would distribute at least five hundred flyers a month and also got paid for other chores around the house. I did small jobs for the neighbors I had met while delivering my dad's marketing flyers. These jobs were easy: cutting lawns, helping paint or haul stuff, pet or house sitting when the neighbors would go out of town.

I never really earned much from any one job, but it's amazing how quickly money in an interest-bearing savings account can increase. If asked, I requested cash gifts for birthdays and Christmas. But after I'd acquired my first car, I found it harder to save, and my banking account started to shrink a little each month.

Many of my friends didn't have this problem because their parents bought them a car and gave them the money for gas and upkeep. They also provided them with cash to do the things they wanted to do. Not my parents! My dad said, "You're not doing any more, so you're not getting any more." It was his belief that learning to earn or do without was a valuable lesson and it was his job to teach it to me. He suggested I go out and sell my skills.

I went to a local restaurant owner I knew and asked if he had any marketing material or flyers that he wanted distributed throughout the neighborhood. He said no because he ran ads in the newspaper. After discussing with him what he paid for an advertisement, its size, and his return on investment (the number of people who came as a result of his ad), I suggested that he advertise instead in a marketing flyer I would create and distribute to a thousand houses right around his restaurant.

In the following three days, I sold a total of eight similar ads because that's how many would fit on both sides of a sheet of paper. The buyers were the local cleaners, a photographer, a loan broker, a roofing company, and a few other local businesses. Each ad cost fifty dollars. I made four hundred dollars minus the cost of printing, which was only fifty dollars. Each business supplied the artwork. It worked out well for them because their advertisement was not hidden in a newspaper but was delivered to the front door of their target market. When their sales went up, the business owners knew it was from my marketing flyer.

It all happened because my sales pitch was my personal declaration. I would walk in and say, "I need money for gas, and I'm saving for college. I'm here to help you get more business if you will give me a chance." That summer Young Entrepreneurial Services (Y.E.S Group Marketing) was born. I had to hire my twelve-year-old sister and some of our friends to help me. I was able to give them jobs and pay them ten to twelve cents apiece. As a matter of fact, my dad had to pay me more per piece because I was so busy with repeat and new orders. He couldn't believe how much money I made that summer, over five thousand dollars.

Anything is possible if you have the correct personal declaration.

Chapter Six
Adjust

Webster's Definition
Adjust: To change as to match or fit. To bring into proper relationship. To conform or adapt as to new conditions.

My Definition
Adjust: Spend more time on goal-related actions or change your goals.

☼

If your priorities are not in line with the goal you want, then something needs to change. If you find yourself spending money rather than saving, playing video games rather than studying, or playing with your friends rather than volunteering, your actions don't reflect your goals and you will need to adjust the course on which you are headed.

Review the commitment dates for your goals and subgoals. Check off those you have accomplished and continue to work toward those you have yet to achieve. The goals you have yet to check off may be too big. Break them down into even smaller goals. Ask for help from your circle of influence, which consists of your family, friends, teachers, counselors, and so on. Through their experiences, they will be able to offer insight that will allow you to develop more achievable goals.

Once you've figured out what those smaller goals are and how to reach them, you will be on the way to completing the original larger goal, which ultimately is to graduate debt-free.

Depending on your level of commitment, you will need to repeat this review process quarterly or even monthly. Adjusting your goals is an ongoing process. If you recognize you are not succeeding, make the change!

Assignment #6:

Get a piece of paper and at the top write Personal Journal. For one week, record all of your activities hour by hour. This exercise will show you where you are spending your time. When the week is complete, analyze your journal entries and ask yourself questions such as these.
- What time did you wake up in the morning?
- What did you do for lunch?
- How did you spend time out of the classroom?
- Where did you sit while in the classroom?

If you see that you are not spending your time on activities that help you accomplish your goals, prioritize your time more responsibly.

If you are spending your time achieving your subgoals and you feel you still aren't progressing toward the big goal of graduating debt-free, contact me, and we will see what needs to change. If you are doing all the exercises in this workbook, it would surprise me if you weren't moving in the right direction.

Chapter Seven
Persist

Webster's Definition
Persist: To be tenacious. To hold steadfastly and firmly to a purpose, state, or undertaking, despite obstacles, warnings, or setbacks.

My Definition
Persist: Get 'er done.

> *"Debt will prohibit me from experiencing the freedom of success."*
> —John D. Lane IV

In high school I established the goal of graduating from college debt-free in four years, in part because I knew that a debt on my parents was a debt on me.

What I am suggesting is not hard!

It starts with taking school seriously. The harder I pushed myself in education, the more I saw myself graduating from a four-year university. Receiving my high school diploma was not a big deal for me because there was no doubt in my mind that I would be graduating from college debt-free. I was much prouder of walking down the aisle, receiving my college degree, and shaking the university president's hand. Both are great accomplishments, but I want you to understand the importance that if you are being real with yourself, it will lead you to higher levels of achievement.

The faster you establish your dreams, the earlier you become determined to accomplish your goals, the easier it will become for you to succeed. Know your priorities. As I shared with you earlier in this workbook, whether it was selling golf balls, lemonade, candy, advertisement space, or marketing for various businesses, I worked. I live by the motto, "Work hard and play hard." I worked through middle school, high school, and college so that I would be able to pay for the privilege of going to school. I did not want to be burdened paying back student loans to XYZ Company, so I saved a lot of what I earned. In the end, my goal was realized.

This workbook will help any young adult who applies its principles the opportunity to graduate debt-free.

Honestly, if you can look me in the eyes and tell me that you have:
- Strived to get A's in all your classes
- Shared your big goal with everyone you know and made them aware of the sacrifices you are making to achieve your big goal
- Worked and saved a portion of your income to apply to the expenses of your first few years of college
- Volunteered for various organizations that also want to see you succeed
- Written out and memorized your personal declaration so it becomes a part of you
- Gone through all the assignments on a monthly basis

I guarantee …

... You will not fail!

My personal guarantee is if you work through the assignments on a monthly basis for the first year and a few times a year after that, by the time you are a senior, you will have enough in the bank to get you through your first year of college. Start early and do everything that is laid out in this workbook, and you will be well on your way to graduating from college debt-free.

Don't give up!